A SHORT ACCOUNT OF THE HINDU SYSTEM OF MUSIC

A SHORT ACCOUNT OF THE HINDU SYSTEM OF MUSIC

ANNE C. WILSON

(A. C. MACLEOD)

AUTHOR OF 'AFTER FIVE YEARS IN INDIA' ETC.

GYAN

Published by

Gyan Publishing House
5, Ansari Road
Daryaganj, New Delhi-110002
Phone: 011-47034999, 9811692060
E-mail: books@gyanbooks.com

Distribution Network
gyanbooks.com
India, USA, Canada, UK, Australia, France

ISBN: 978-81-212-7174-5 (PB)

First Published, 1904

2nd Impression 2024

Printed at: Gyan Press, Delhi.

A SHORT ACCOUNT OF THE HINDU SYSTEM OF MUSIC
Author: ANNE C. WILSON

THE HINDU SYSTEM OF MUSIC

THE HINDU SYSTEM OF MUSIC

I Propose in the following pages to unfold some of the intricacies of the Indian system of music. Before doing so, it may be interesting to my readers to have an account of how one's interest in Indian music was first awakened, and of how my knowledge of it, such as it is, was acquired.

During many years spent in India, our winters have been chiefly passed in camp, wandering from one part of the district to another, or latterly from place to place in the bigger world of the Province. It has always been an ambition and pleasure to us, as to other Indian officials and their families, to try, as far as possible, to bridge the gulf which must ever separate the Eastern and Western races, and which exists, as a matter of fact, between each Indian household and its neighbour.

This is by no means easy: first of all because it must be granted that human nature, although it shares some elemental instincts with every living thing, is not the same the whole world over. If we are to know our Indian neighbour as he is, we can make no deductions from our own sensations as to what his may be. We have to learn not so much to put ourselves in his place, as to try to understand him in his own.

The attempt is almost hopeless when dealing with a people whose traditions, customs, mental bias, and inherent attitude towards life are so different from our own. Our efforts, moreover, are not simplified through the unguarded self-revelation of those with whom we come in contact. With franker manners superficially, our fellow subjects are in the last resort more reticent than we are. In no country more than in India can it with greater truth be said, that each man lives and dies alone, hardly trusting to the members of his own household the secret purport of his heart.

The inner life of the people of India is for us eternally enveloped in mystery. We see only the surface of their life and from that alone can attempt to draw our inferences. Like children searching for something hidden in their game, who look for it, and hope that some indication in the outward aspects of things may lead them to the object of their search, so we pursue our quest, and watch the panorama of Eastern daily life, trusting that we may catch some hint of the elusive mystery underlying it, the secret essence of its motive power, which for ever escapes our grasp.

A paternal Government knows little of the home life of its children. Our system of administration, by a political necessity, leaves the private idiosyncrasies of the people of India untouched. As long as prince or pauper observes certain laws he is allowed to pursue his own existence in his own time-worn way, while we remain outside of it and in another world.

We meet, it is true, under varied circumstances; but has any European ever seen the other side of the shield, any more than an inhabitant of earth has ever viewed the other side of the moon? The civilian spends part, perhaps, of every day in the fields, where the peasants watch the earth beneath and sky above them, where they sow and reap and wrest their uttermost from nature as they have done from immemorial ages. At other times, in his capacity as judge, he is in courts of justice, to which they bring their histories of loves, hatreds, hereditary feuds, and crimes. Sometimes he has lengthy interviews with those who wish to have a grievance remedied, a burden removed, or an honour bestowed. When evening comes he may wander through the bazaar and view the history of the Hindu pantheon painted in crude colours round a shop, or find a stray specimen of indigenous literature, which gives the history of a Mohammedan or Sikh saint and throws some light on their religious aspirations. He may see all the necessities of their daily life in process of production, and study their household goods, pictures, jewels, toys, displayed upon the stalls which hold the odds and ends of their aesthetics. He may see every splash of vivid paint which is daubed upon the palette to make the portrait of their life. But does he know the living sitters any better at the end of his long day than he did at the beginning ?

Speaking for ourselves we cannot boast of success. On lands where golden fields of wheat spoke of the prosperity of the owners, we have been the guests of Mohammedan and Hindu gentlemen, whose wives I have visited, holding their babies in my arms and playing with their girls and boys. In lonely tracts of country we have visited the tents and caves of jungle tribes, talked to the famine-stricken, strayed through leper villages, interviewed cattle-trackers, lizard-hunters, fortune-tellers by the score. By our camp fire at night we have had strange visitors, poets who recited their own fervent jingles, philosophers who expounded the tenets of their sects, performing troupes of actors, jugglers, story-tellers, and astrologers. Who has ever known the romance of life in camp without having some experiences such as these, and with the same result ?

At the end of many years, we have known we could repeat all that we had seen and heard, as glibly as we might repeat the words and grammar of a language, of which we had still failed to grasp the inherent and essential meaning.

From all of these experiences music was for a long time excluded. Once or twice, when a band of native musicians came, sat in a row on the ground with their drums, violins, or pipes, and essayed a performance, the experiment proved unfortunate, and seemed to me synonymous with pandemonium. The discordant yells of men, whose appearance suggested the extremities of toothache on their part, tended to induce insanity on mine.

Several years passed without anything occurring to dislodge my prejudices or alter my opinion, until one evening I heard a man playing in a field beside our tent. He was playing a violin with a drummer beating an accompaniment, and as I listened I thought I had never heard anything more beautiful. It reminded me of the music one hears in the Highlands of Scotland, which are like stories told with only the hills to hear them until they become a song; or of the melodies I had heard gipsies sing in Spain; or the wild airs Hungarians improvise. But this was sadder even than these, fuller of a monotonous despair, as if it carried in it the burden of the world's woe, and was the voice of the old and endless 'still sad music of humanity.'

We sent someone to find out who the player was, and learned he was a man whose days were chiefly spent sitting by the grave of a renowned Mohammedan saint, whose shrine was visited by crowds, to whom this man was accustomed to perform.

He came and played to us, and as I sat listening to him under a clump of trees, with dark fields of wheat before me, and beyond a stretch of barren, arid plain, which met at last the starlit sky, it seemed to me that I had at last discovered the hidden secret I had sought for years, and that this was the unconscious expression of the heart of the people.

The mysteries of man's nature are perhaps in the last resort incommunicable, sometimes unknown to himself, only recognised in a dumb way by others. But if they have a language, it is surely in music, the most immaterial of all arts. As I listened, I seemed for the first time to know something of the inner world about me. I heard in the music the history of vague longings after the unseen and the eternal, the dull resignation to unalterable fate. Then there came strains of vigorous cheerfulness and rustic humour, alternating with hysterical emotion, feverish passion, undisciplined excitement, hatred and despair, and then again monotony and enduring hopelessness. To me it seemed that evening as if the dumb had found a voice, and deaf ears had gained the power of hearing. Gulab Mahomed remained with us a week, and during the ensuing years he had many successors as visitors to our camp. Musicians were our neighbours wherever we went, as every village in the Punjab contains some of the Mirasi caste to which these men belong. For, as we now learnt, the people of India are essentially a musical race. As amongst the Highlanders of Scotland and the peasantry of Russia, every important event in their life has its appropriate song. To such an extent is music an accompaniment of existence in India, that every hour of the day and season of the year has its own melody. Mirasis wander about the Punjab like the bards and minstrels of the middle ages. They are amongst the retinues of the great, and are employed by them to celebrate the births and marriages of their children, or to sing the praises of their ancestors or themselves. The Mirasi wiles away some idle hours with lengthy ballads, relating perhaps the loves of Hir and Ranjha, Soni and Maiwal, or it may be with the battle songs of kings, beginning with those of Alexander, by sea or land. He sings hymns in honour of some well-known saint, he composes a lampoon on his patron's enemy or eulogises his defeat. It is he who sings his patron's dirge.

In Indian villages Mirasis are equally prominent. If they do not wield the power of the pen, they possess the poet's capacity to bless or curse, and patronage and flattery are pretty equally divided between audience and performer, while the artist sells his talents at excellent profit. At marriages, fairs, and religious festivals they are in great request: in everyday life they figure largely in the foreground. Mirasi women are called in upon various occasions, as, for instance, to invoke the aid of the goddess Sitala if a child is sick, to sing a friend away when she leaves the village, or to welcome her with a song on her return. The farmer listens to the enumeration of his cattle's attributes, or to a skit upon some local celebrity. If there is nothing new to hear, it is always possible to fall back on abiding songs of love-lorn women and deserted wives, some of the saddest of all being those describing the sorrows of girls when they marry, leave their early homes and bid their parents farewell.

Of course music in India, as in all countries, is distinctly unequal in quality. *Rags,* as they are called, while limited by certain laws and regulations, are improvised at the sweet will of the singer. Consequently they may frequently prove to be 'excessively uninspired.' On these occasions, however, recalling the words of the French poem,

> Il faut que nous nous disions Adieu,
> Parce que nous ne marchons pas sur le meme chemin,

it is always possible to end the concert.

At other times, and they are not amongst the least enjoyable, it may happen that, owing to the alien time of the music, the great length of the phrases, and the multiplication of quarter and half tones, one finds it quite impossible to follow or grasp the composition as a whole or attempt to reproduce it. But this does not mitigate one's appreciation of its weird character and beauty, just as it would not detract from our delight in some undreamt-of atmospheric effect, if we knew that it could never be transferred by us to canvas.

On the whole it is more enjoyable to hear the song played than sung. The women modulate their voices as a rule, but the Mirasi man has powerful lungs, and it is the tradition of the uneducated to exercise them in singing with inconsiderate unrestraint.

A characteristic peculiarity of the phrasing which must never be forgotten, and which also adds to one's difficulty in following it, is that each note is merged in the next. If there is a wide interval between one note and its successor, grace notes lead from the first to the second, and unite them. The passage generally ends with a long vibrating note which the people themselves colloquially describe as 'machhi mar katan'—'vibrating like a bird above the water before it pounces on its prey'—which introduces an element of uncertainty into one's sense of time.

I mention these facts as a prelude to saying that no one who is attracted by Indian music—and this I believe an ever-increasing number of our fellow countrymen to be—need hope to disentangle its mysteries at once. During seven winters spent in camp, I learnt but a very little, and that at long intervals and from various and unexpected sources. At one time a Brahmin pandit was my teacher, at another a discharged policeman who had reverted to his old profession as a wandering musician. A third preceptor was a rather incoherent priest. He explained to us quite frankly that he was the victim of drugs, and his nerves and powers of endurance were so quickly worn out under cross-examination, that we soon heard him audibly beg a bystander 'for the love of heaven to get his horse saddled quickly to take him out of this.'

The greater proportion of people, who sing and play according to the traditions of their system, cannot explain its principles, and have not the mental tenacity of purpose required for its elucidation. It is only recently, and within the comparatively short period of four months, that I have been able to get at the root of its difficulties and master its construction, under the guidance and tuition of Pandit Vishnu Digambar, Principal of the Lahore School of Music. It was only after his illuminating instruction, and with the essential accessory of a piano, that I have been able to transcribe the few examples of *rags, ragnis,* and *putras* I have appended to the account of the system of Indian music which follows this introduction.

My hope is that others may begin where I end, that they may add flesh and blood to the bare skeleton I present; my certainty is that they would find in the attempt its own reward.

Wearied by the day's hard work, with few distractions to lead them to forget it, they have only to summon another Gulab Mohamed to be a David to their Saul, to transport them to another world, to reconcile them to the world around them. For there, behind the disappointments which confront us on its surface, they will know its soul, they will understand its sorrows, they will pity its irreconcilable and conflicting temperament, they will wait in patience for its deliverance.

This then is what I claim for Indian music, that more than anything else in India it is a revelation of the people from whom it springs. 'True folk music,' as Sir Hubert Parry writes, 'is an outcome of the whole man, as is the case with all that is really valuable in art. The features which give it its chief artistic and historical importance, apart from its general delightfulness, are those in which the emotional and intellectual basis of art is illustrated by the qualities of the tunes which correspond with the known character of the nations and people who invent them. Highly sensitive races express themselves with high degrees of emotional force and variety of form; placid races show perfect content in simple design with little meaning, races of moderate intelligence, who have considerable skill in manipulation and love of effect, introduce much ornamentation; serious and strong races, and those with much reserve of disposition, produce very simple and dignified tunes; and so on in various degrees.

'The very fact of musical utterance implies a genuine expansion of the nature of the human being, and is in varying degree a trustworthy revelation of the particular likings and. tastes and sensibilities of the being or groups of beings that give vent to it.'

One word in conclusion. Some of us may remember books for children, which were in vogue many years ago, in which information was attempted to be conveyed through the medium of fictitious conversations between a mother and her children. Among the questioners there was always a stupid one—I think her name was generally Emma—who endeared herself to me by asking the most obvious questions, which, however, enlightened me on the very points which were puzzling my own brain.

I have tried as far as possible to remember Emma's difficulties, in the following pages, and to be as plain and explicit in my explanations as it was possible to be, and must apologise for this to those who could have dispensed with all vain repetitions and unnecessary details. I have written them for Emma's friends !

The Hindu Notes of the Scale

That passion for continuity which is innate in us all, and shown in its most elemental form in our pride in long descent, in our desire for descendants, in our dreams of fame, in our instincts for immortality, exists in a marked degree in the Hindu races. It must, therefore, be a secret source of pride to them to know that their system of music, as a written science, is the oldest in the world. Its principal features were given long ago in Vedic writings. Its laws were orally transmitted from an age dating many centuries before our Christian era, and were carried through all the intervening centuries, accepted by the Mohammedan portion of the population in the days of their pre-eminence, and are still in use in their original construction at the present day.

To some of my readers, whose associations with Indian music are darkened by memories of multitudes of half-tones, which to our ears seem only out of tune, it may be a matter of surprise to learn that the Hindu scale has seven notes in it corresponding very closely to those of our own scale, and that this scale has existed since Vedic ages.

Let me give a more particular account of the Hindu scale, commencing with its pedigree! For the Hindus, with their love of allegory and of personifying inanimate objects, describe the scale in the following manner:—

Sound is called vadh. Out of sound proceed srutis. Their home is in the heart, throat, or head (according as they come in the lower, middle, or upper part of the scale).

The srutis merge into or produce the completed note called swar.

Git (song) is the child of swar and the parent of instrumental music.

Leaving the srutis undisturbed in their home at present, I shall confine myself to a more elaborate introduction of the notes (swar), giving them under all their different titles and symbols, whether in Sanskrit or English characters, and presenting these in a table in the following order :—

Table giving the Hindu and English names of the Swar.

Hindu name in Roman characters	Common Abbreviation written in Roman characters	European name of note	Sanskrit sign or notation	European Equivalent
Kharja (Shudja) [1]	Sa	C	सा	
Rishaba . .	Re	D	रे	
Gandhara . .	Ga	E	गा	
Madhyama .	Ma	F	मा	
Panchama .	Pa	G	पा	
Dhaivata . .	Dha	A	धा	
Nishada . .	Ni	B	नी	

1. Sa, as having the initial letter of Swar, is used for the tonic note of the scale instead of Kharja (Shudja).

Hindu Quarter-notes

And now to analyse still more closely the composition of the Hindu scale.

A Hindu scale is composed of 22 srutis, and what these are I must now explain. We have seen that there are seven swar or notes in a Hindu scale exactly corresponding to the seven notes of our scale. But between each of our whole tones or semitones the Hindu scale has quarter-tones and the third of a tone, and these are called srutis. These minute intervals are not mathematically equal, but are equal in practice, and are allotted to the several notes in the following order:—

Sa	Re	Ga	Ma	Pa	Dha	Ni
4	3	2	4	4	3	2

Carl Engel, in his 'Introduction to the Study of National Music,' represents these subdivisions in this way:—

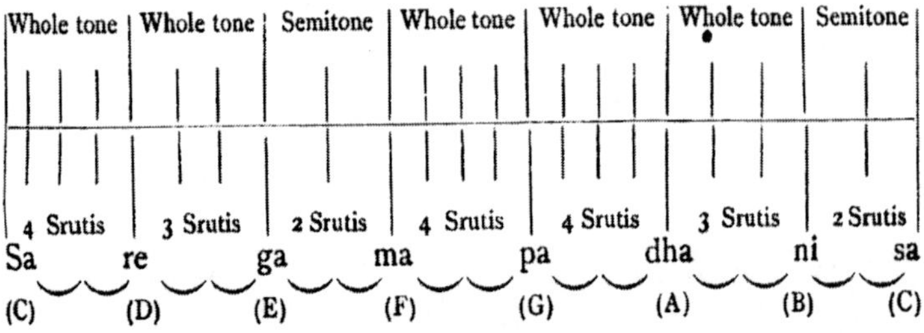

I shall now give a table with the Hindu names and signs for these notes and half-notes. These notes are to be found in old Sanskrit books, and had formerly the same meaning as is now attached to them. The signs are modern, and are those used for the purposes of notation by Pandit Vishnu Digambar, Principal of the Hindu School of Music in Lahore, who has given me a great deal of fresh information about Indian music and confirmed or corrected all I had previously been able to gather.

Sign of Note	Sanskrit name written in Roman characters	Translation
	Shudh	Natural
	Komal	Half-note
	Atti komal	Quarter-note
	Tibre	Quarter-note before a sharp
	Tibre tar	Sharp
	Tibre tam	Quarter-note above a sharp

It is these quarter-tones and thirds of a tone in Indian airs which are so alien to our unaccustomed ears, although we hear them daily in the songs of birds and can reproduce them on the violin. It may interest the reader to hear the attempt to justify their musical existence, made by an enthusiast for Indian music, who wrote in the beginning of last century—although it must be noticed that Captain Willard does not personally commit himself to their appreciation. He says: 'To a person versed in the modern music of Europe, the sub-divisions of semitones into minuter parts will appear incomprehensible, at least inasmuch as to be productive of any melody that would be pleasing to the ear. I shall forbear to say anything on my own authority but shall quote a passage which I think appropriate:—

'Dr. Burney, in his general dissertation on the music of the ancients, treating of the Greek enharmonic genus says:—"How the quarter-tone could be managed so as to be rendered pleasing still remains a mystery. Yet the difficulty of splitting a semi-tone into two halves or even dividing it into more minute intervals, is less perhaps than has been imagined. When it is practised by a capital singer or a good performer on the violin or hautbois, at a pause, how wide it seems!"

'T. Moore, in his translation of the "XLIII. Ode of Anacreon," has the following note:—

' "One of their modes was a progression by quarter-notes, which we are told was the nature of the enharmonic scale. Simplicity was by no means the characteristic of their melody; for this is a nicety of progression, of which modern music is incapable."

'That such subdivisions exist in Hindustanee music is certain, but it must be left to time, and more intimate acquaintance with the science, to determine whether it has any claims to the eulogium bestowed by this gentleman on the enharmonic of the Greeks.'[1]

For those to whom these subdivisions are anathema, it may be some consolation to learn that many Indian airs are composed wholly on the notes with which we are already familiar, and that, granting them their own peculiar rhythm, they can be played and sung by us as if they were entirely English! Whatever our attitude towards the other and more characteristic Indian melodies may be, it will always be impossible for us to transcribe them, as we have no signs for these subdivisions of notes in our musical notation.

The Three Indian Octaves

To proceed with the description of Indian octaves. There are three of these, called saptakas, which all begin on C, and

1. *Treatise on the Music of Hindustanee.* By Captain A. Willard.

are named Tar, Madhya, and Mandra. Here is a table giving the names or signs of the octave in Sanskrit, Roman, and English characters:—

Sanskrit sign	Hindu name in Roman characters	Corresponding in English to
तार	Tar	Treble
मध्य	Madhya	Tenor
मंद्र	Mandra	Bass

The same intervals exist in all three octaves just as they do in our own scale, the intervals in one octave being as follows:—

$$\text{Sa} + \tfrac{1}{8} = \text{re} \qquad \text{Pa} + \tfrac{1}{8} = \text{dha}$$
$$\text{Re} + \tfrac{1}{8} = \text{ga} \qquad \text{Dha} + \tfrac{1}{4} = \text{ni}$$
$$\text{Ga} + \tfrac{1}{12} = \text{ma} \qquad \text{Ni} + \tfrac{1}{8} = \text{sa}$$
$$\text{Ma} + \tfrac{1}{6} = \text{pa}$$

Notation of Indian Octaves

The next two diagrams illustrate the notation of Indian octaves, the first being given in Roman characters, the second in Sanskrit characters.

Tar	sa	re	ga	ma	pa	dha	ni
Madhya	sa	re	ga	ma	pa	dha	ni
Mandra	sa	re	ga	ma	pa	dha	ni

तार	सा	रे	गा	मा	पा	धा	नी
मध्य	सा	रे	गा	मा	पा	धा	नी
मंद्र	सा	रे	गा	मा	पा	धा	नी

In order to show how the notes of an air are written in the spaces belonging to the three octaves, I shall transcribe the last line of 'Home, Sweet Home' in Sanskrit and Roman characters, giving the same notes in our notation, with the time omitted in each instance.

Tar		sa सा											
Madhya	pa प		ni नी	dha धा	pa प	pa प	ga ग	pa प	pa प	dha धा	ma म	re रे	sa सा
Mandra													

Hindu Views on Harmony

It will be seen that no space in these diagrams is occupied by chords, for the simple reason that they are never sung; although the use of certain words in Sanskrit such as

Vadi	principal note
Samvadi	note harmonising with it
Anuvadi	note subordinate to it
Vivadi	discordant

shows that some of the most elemental rules of harmony were at least understood by musicians in Vedic ages.

A Hindu gentleman, wishing to convey to me the meaning he attached to these words, said Vadi was like the Nawab of a great kingdom, Samvadi was his Wazir with whom he agreed,

Anuvadi was the Wazir's secretary. When all three were of one mind the agreement was still more perfect. Vivadi was like a discordant element coming in.

There are certain other indications that some such rudimentary principles of harmony are recognised, and in some instances put in practice.

For instance, the drum which accompanies singing is capable of sounding all the notes of the scale C D E F G A B, but the rule is that it may only sound C F G, and that C and G may be played together  or C and F  but never C G F 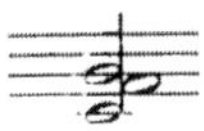 as that would be discord.

Hindus also dwell on the fact, when allegorically defining the relations between the different notes of the scale, that C is connected with every note in the gamut, but more especially with G, or in a less degree with F.

D and A are closely connected.

D and G in a lesser degree.

E and B are closely connected.

E with A, and F with C and B in a lesser degree.

A glance at these chords in their written form will furnish the best illustration of those Indian views on harmony :

Whether the constant return to the keynote in Indian music indicates any feeling after harmony, I must leave it to those, who are more conversant with the laws of the science than I am, to decide.

It may be of interest in this connexion to give the criticisms made by Ambrose on some Indian airs, published by W. Hamilton Bird in 1789:—'Auffallend ist in den von den englischen Sammlern aufnotirten Melodien das deutliche Gefühl für die gewählte Grundtonart, für die Eigenheit der Dominante den Gang der melodischen Perioden an gehöriger Stelle, mit einem Halbschlusse zu markiren, für die Bedeutung und Schlusskraft der Tonika, für melodischen Zusammenhang im Periodenbau, wie in consequenter Führung eines für die Melodie vollig gewählten thematischen Motives; häufig begegnet man Melodieabsätzen von vier zu vier Takten, oft auch scheidet sich eine Melodie völlig leidmässig in einen ersten und zweiten Theil, oder dreitheilig, mit erstem, zweitem und drittem (dem ersten analogen) Theil, was nachstehende Proben bewähren mögen.'[1]

Meaning of certain Words used in Hindu Musical Vocabulary

When a Hindu musician is talking about a scale or an air he often uses certain words, which it may be well to give here with their explanation.

One is aroha, ascending; the other is its opposite, avaroha, descending.

A third word is grama. I shall take the liberty of quoting Raja Tagore's explanation of this word, and of giving what

1. *Geschichte der Musik.*

he calls 'the popular version of the function of the three gramas.'[1]

From his account of the three, it would seem that they are no other than our three scales of (1) C, (2) E with four sharps, and (3) F with one flat. I offer this explanation with diffidence, however, as mystery and many differences of opinion usually hover round the word grama.

Raja Tagore writes: 'There are three gramas in Hindu music, viz. : the Sa grama, the Ga grama, and the Ma grama. The reason why the three notes Sa, Ga, and Ma, and no others, have been selected to represent the three gramas is that it is the scales of these three notes which between them furnish, to use the language of the pianoforte, the seven white keys and the five black keys of the diapason. Thus:

'When Sa (C) is made the keynote, the seven white keys are obtained, viz.: Sa (C), Ri (D), Ga (E), Ma (F), Pa (G), Dha (A), Ni (B).

'When Ga (E) is the keynote, four of the black notes are obtained, viz.: Ma (F) sharp, Dha (A) flat, Ri (D) flat, Ga (E) flat.[2]

'When Ma (F) is made the keynote, the fifth black is obtained viz.: Ni (B) flat'

Always remember that the keynote is called Sa in every case, just as in our Do, re, me system we invariably call the keynote Do.

---

1. Appendix to *Universal History of Music*, by Raja Sir Sourindro Mohun Tagore, &c.
2. We should call all of these notes sharp, *i.e.* F sharp, G sharp, C sharp, D sharp, the four sharps in the scale of E.

Another word which is often used in connexion with scales or airs is murchhana. Sometimes this means that the voice is run from one note to another of the scale either ascending or descending it, the Sanskrit definition being that it is the orderly (gradual) ascent or descent of the seven notes of the scale. At other times it is the name given to that vibration on a note, sometimes long and sometimes short, which is such a well-known characteristic of Hindu music. How often one has heard it in the stillness of the night, when some travellers from the far-off hills to the distant plains, wandering along the dusty roads in solitude, wards off ghosts and evil spirits, and strives perhaps to pass the time by a song, that to the wakeful listener seems the essence of the spirit of loneliness and hopeless grief. Then the murchhana quavers on the high notes, and vibrates on the low ones like a broken sob.

Hindu Measure of Time

To return, however, to the discussion of the framework of Indian music. Let me take it for granted that the reader has learnt what to expect, so far as the mere notes of it are concerned, when he settles himself down to listen to Indian music, and that he is able to recognise the existence of the notes of his own scale, side by side with others which are infinitesimally different from them. I should expect that one of the first things he would further notice would be, how different the rhythm of the music often was from ours, how much longer the phrases were, how irregular the lilt. It would seem, to compare it with poetry, as if he were hearing for the first time an entirely unknown metre; or, to compare it with speech, as if he were listening to a human being, who, under the spell of intensified feeling, spoke now in short sentences, now with an impassioned cry, and again with a volume of words full of that magnetism which overpowering passion imparts.

He would also notice that the beat of the accompaniment was regulated by some mysterious law, which was equally new to him.

But if, disregarding these novel characteristics of rhythm and accompaniment, he were to analyse the time of the bars beaten by the hands of some of the audience, he would discover, probably to his surprise, that it was exactly the same as our own, just as he would find that the orthodox numbers of crotchets were used in the triple time of some wild fandango, esquidilla, or bolero of Spain, although the fact were disguised or obscured by the rhythm in which the notes were played.

And in this discovery he would find the true state of the case. Just as in the old Sanskrit treatises on music the names of our seven notes of the octave and of sharps and naturals are given, so too in these old books the names for the equivalent of our semibreve, minim, crotchets, quavers, and semiquavers are given also, and had the same meaning in ancient times as they now possess. The timetable of those ages was practically the same as our own, and was in use in India thousands of years before it was completely accepted in Europe.

Hindus take the crotchet as the unit of time as we do, marking the time by beating their hands. The length of the crotchet, they say, is equal to a second, and for every second they beat once.

A minim is equal to two crotchets, and should therefore be given two beats, each of the same length as a crotchet.

A semibreve is equal to four beats, each of the same length as a crotchet.

A quaver, on the other hand, is half the length of a crotchet. So two quavers go to one beat, while four semiquavers and eight demi-semiquavers are each only equal to one crotchet, and the four and eight respectively go to one beat.

For all of these notes the Hindu name and sign as given in Sanskrit books may be seen in the following diagram, the value of the notes being the same in practice now as they formerly were, and exactly corresponding to the value we give the same notes.

Indian name	English name	Indian sign	English sign	Value of the note relatively to a crotchet in England and India
Chatasr. .	semibreve	X	𝅝	4
Guru . .	minim	~	𝅗𝅥	2
Laghu . .	crotchet	|	♩	1
Drut . .	quaver	•	♪	$\frac{1}{2}$
Anu-drut .	semiquaver	∪	𝅘𝅥𝅯	$\frac{1}{4}$
Anu-anudrut	demisemi-quaver		𝅘𝅥𝅰	$\frac{1}{8}$

Of course the assertion that a crotchet beat lasts for a second of time is purely arbitrary, and the pace at which the music is taken is expressed in India as in England by such times as :—

Velambit, which corresponds to our adagio.

Dugan, which is twice as quick as velambit.

Drut, which is four times as quick as velambit and corresponds to our presto.

Sometimes the singer sings at velambit pace and has his accompaniment played at dugan pace. And sometimes the same air beginning slowly is repeated at dugan pace and finally ends at drut velocity.

Distinction between Practical and Theoretical Knowledge of Indian Music

And here I must pause, and, in order to prevent misunderstandings, make a digression to let the reader clearly grasp the fact that he will not find every one of these definitions given by the ordinary mass of musicians. A distinction must be made between what is known by every native performer, and the theoretical knowledge of music, which is only possessed by educated people in India.

Every village musician, to give some examples, knows his scale and sings it, calling the notes by the names sa, re, ga, &c. Every village player knows about time, and marks it, by beating time on the ground while the audience clap their hands along with him. He has a most subtle ear for time, and a more delicate perception of shades of difference than the generality of English people can acquire, an acuteness of musical hearing which also makes it possible for him to recognise and reproduce quarter and half tones, when singing or playing.

But while this practical and traditional knowledge exists and has, so to speak, been orally handed down from generation to generation, he does not know music theoretically. It is only educated Hindus who have learnt the principles of Indian music. Of these there are an ever-increasing number. In the Central Provinces, for instance, there are schools : in the capital of Mysore, in Poona, in Madras, in Bankura and Bissempur, and above all in Calcutta, where the Academy of

Music was founded in 1881, by His Highness Raja Tagore,[1] who is himself an enthusiastic exponent of the art. In addition to these schools there are teachers of music, such as the Ustad of Baroda, who is the Court musician of the Gaikwar of that State, and his brother in Nepal, who have, through their publications and personal instructions, pupils in every part of India.

I am told that the system taught in all these places is fundamentally the same. Personally, I am only able to speak of the instruction given by Pandit Vishnu Digambar, Principal of the Lahore School of Music, which I understand corresponds in broad lines with that given by the Ustad of Baroda. Some further particulars of that system I shall now proceed to give.

Our first visit to the Pandit's class-room was a memorable one, for there we saw for the first time a wonderful collection of musical instruments, sarangis, sitars, tambouras, and the most ancient of all these varieties of violin, the vina—this one standing on feet, which gave it the air of a large wooden grasshopper; another like a gigantic banjo; a third resembling a Spanish mandoline; while various drummers sat beside their dhols, tablas, and dholkis ready to make the low roof echo with their rattling beat. Here, too, we heard for the first time a Vedic hymn, composed in prehistoric times and in character reminding one partly of a German chorale, partly of a Gregorian chant.

---

1. Raja Sir Sourindro Mohun Tagore (Knt.), Mus.D., *honoris causä,* 1896, Oxford, President Bengal Royal Academy of Music, and Bengal Music School, Sangita Nayaka, Calcutta. It is interesting to note that Raja Tagore is the first Oriental of any nation who has had his services to the Art of Music recognised in our universities.

When we went away we carried home with us one of the Pandit's musical primers, which are written in Hindustani and have never been translated, but which he afterwards patiently explained to us, his latest scholars.

Notation of Indian Measure ot Time

I think it may interest my readers to know the system of notation adopted by Pandit Vishnu Digambar, in common with other teachers of Hindu music, in order to make it possible for their pupils not only to transcribe the notes, but also the time of any composition they wish to preserve, an innovation of incalculable advantage in the history of Indian music.

I shall give some illustrations of his method, always taking common time as an example, and placing the same bar in English time underneath. His method, then, consists in taking the ancient Sanskrit signs for semibreves, minims, crotchets, quavers, and semiquavers  and writing them under the notes to signify their time, in this way:—

Hindu signs of crotchet, quavers, and minim:

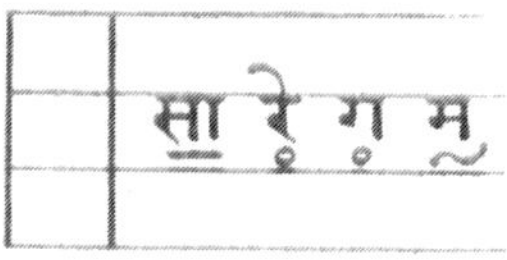

These signs given in European notation :

The sign for a rest is represented by the addition of vertical strokes.

Hindu signs of quavers, crotchet, and semiquaver, each followed by the sign of the rest:

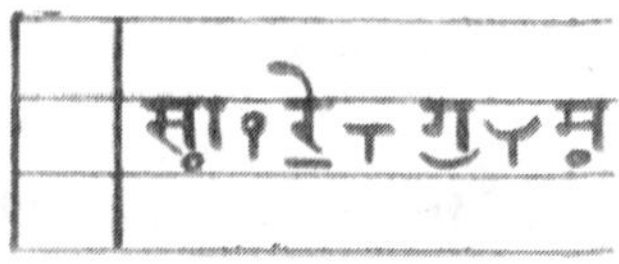

These signs given in European notation:

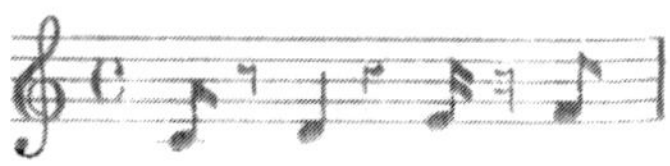

Where we should, by the use of a slur,  signify that the sound of the note in singing was to be maintained for the duration of the rest indicated, he signifies the same thing by adding a horizontal stroke to the vertical one.

Hindu sign of a sustained minim rest:

A dot after any sign means that the value of that sign is increased by half.

Hindu sign of a minim, a crotchet dot, and a crotchet:

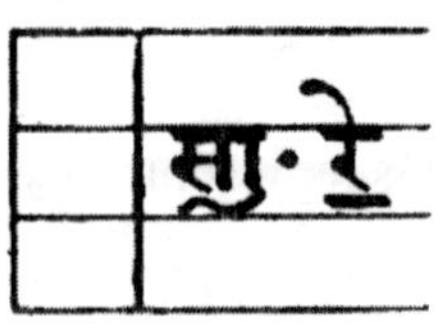

These signs given in European notation:

This system is of immense practical advantage, for it is now for the first time possible for every Indian lover of music to read the notes and the time of any composition, without being dependent, as in old days, upon learning them by ear. But it must again be emphasised, that while the signs used in Sanskrit notation have been thus utilised and adapted for present-day use, so bringing it within the power of every modern musician to transcribe his music in Sanskrit characters, the custom of centuries is still the only one in use with most of the illiterate musicians. The village singer's only knowledge of time is in his ear and foot, even his toes marking the time, the rests, and pauses as he squats on the ground, while the listening audience clap their hands in their immemorial manner, just as the leader of a choir at home would keep his choir together with his bâton.

Hindu Rags

And now to give a short account of the music which is sung by the people of India. The year is divided by Hindus into six seasons. Each season has its own rag, respectively called—

Bhairau	Sirirag
Hindola	Dipak
Megh	Malkaus.

The Hindus, with their love of allegory and of personifying inanimate objects, say that every rag is a demigod wedded to five ragnis and is father to eight genii, called putra or sons, expressing by this imagery the fact, that every one of the six rags has associated with it five ragnis and eight putras, the six rags and thirty ragnis being more widely sung than the putras.

Having assigned to each season its rag, the Hindus next divide the day into six parts, and give to each division its particular rag.

Bhairau is sung from 4 A.M. till 8 A.M.

Hindola from 8 A.M. till 12 noon.

Megh from 12 noon till 4 P.M.

Sirirag from 4 P.M. till 8 P.M.

Dipak from 8 P.M. till 12 midnight.

Malkaus from 12 midnight till 4 A.M.

The people say that only at that time has the presiding Deity of the rag leisure to listen to it; but it cannot be denied that they occasionally sing it at other times too, when they have leisure to enjoy it themselves. There are other exceptions, besides those which are self-imposed, to the general rule of rigidly adhering to the appropriate hour of each rag. 'In the month of Phagan (February and March) any rag,' says a Hindu writer, 'may be sung at every hour of the day and night, and in Basant (spring) the same is the case; but a respite of one hour in the night should be given'—a concession for which even the greatest enthusiast for Indian music and Indian drummers can hardly be ungrateful! In its own season, also, the rag is not confined to any particular hour of the day or night, although Megh is the only one which, as a matter of fact, is continually heard in its own season—the period of rain—for the very good reason that its notes are supposed to have a mystical power of attracting the longed-for clouds and beneficent rains. Roughly speaking, however, the people consider it unlucky or inappropriate to sing a rag out of the hour allotted to it in the course of the day.

Law as to Notes used in the Rags

Certain notes must be used in each rag and no other: they are the necessary notes of that particular rag. The singer improvises when he uses them. He sings at his own sweet will, but there are certain notes (vadi, anuvadi, and samvadi) which must be made prominent, and he must adhere to certain sequences of notes. With these exceptions he can invent as he pleases, provided he uses only the notes belonging to that particular rag.

From this it follows that the rendering of the same rag in different parts of the country by different singers will differ in detail. The notes will be the same, but their disposition will be entirely different, although the same general effect must be produced. To this principle of eternal improvising, some popular airs, such as ' Taza-bataza,' which is composed on the notes of the ragni Sham Kalyan, and others, form an exception, being known and sung in one way throughout India.

Number of Notes used in the Rag

But not only must the musician stick to the use of certain notes in each separate rag; he must adhere to the prescribed number of notes. The Hindus, with their peculiar love of giving a name to every imaginable subdivision of any given object, have found a word for any and every number of notes that could be used in a composition. If only one note were struck the name would be Archik; if two, Gatik; if three, Samik; if four, Swaranter. As, however, never less than five notes are employed in performing the rags, the only terms of any practical importance are:

Orav	the name given when five notes are used.
Sharav	when six notes are used.
Sampooran	when seven notes are used.

So far four facts have to be borne in mind about a rag—(1) its name; (2) the hour at which it is played; (3) the notes used in it; (4) their number.

I shall now give examples of the six rags in which this information is furnished.

Name of rag	Hour at which it is sung	Number of notes in rag	Notes on which rag begins	Note on which rag ends	Principal note	Notes of rag
Bhairau .	4 A.M. till 8 A.M.	7 Sampooran		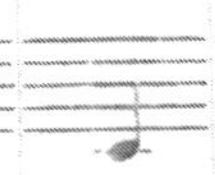		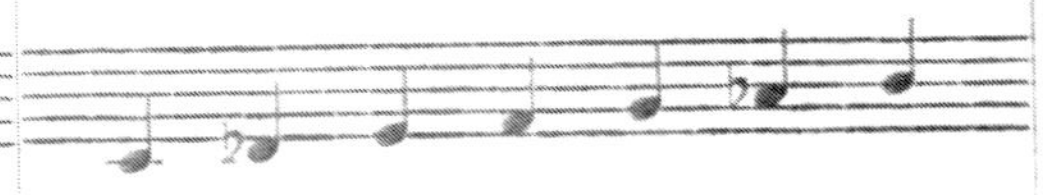
Hindola .	8 A.M. till 12 noon	5 Orav .			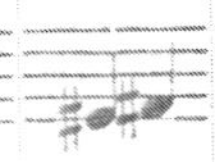	
Megh .	12 noon till 4 P.M.	7 Sampooran		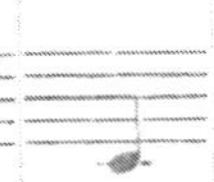		
Sirirag .	4 P.M. till 8 P.M.	7 Sampooran		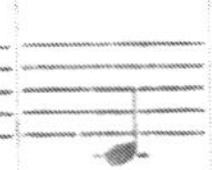		
Dipak .	8 P.M. till 12 midnight	7 Sampooran				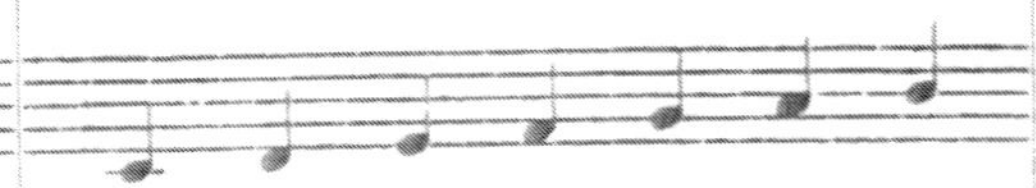
Malkaus .	12 midnight till 4 A.M.	5 Orav .				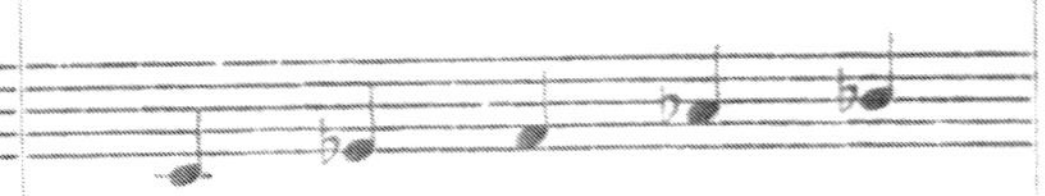

Specimens of rags, ragnis, and putras. The first rag was dictated by Pandit Vishnu Digambar. The other specimens of rags, ragnis, and putras were collected from village musicians in the Punjab.

Air written on the notes of the rag Bhairau.

Air written on the notes of the rag Megh.

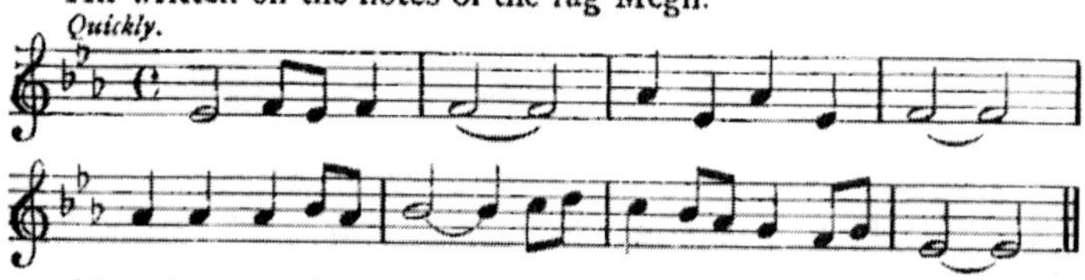

Air written on the notes of the rag Malkaus.

Air written on the notes of Bhairavin, a ragni of Bhairau.

Air written on the notes of Asavari, a ragni of Sirirag.

Air written on the notes of Kaliam, a putra of Dipak.

Air written on the notes of Gawra, a putra of Dipak.

Further Classification of the Rags

It will be noticed that some rags have only flats, that others have only sharps, that C and G are always natural, &c.

To embrace these distinctions a further and final classification has been made. Under one or other of the six following heads, every rag, ragni, and putra that exists can find its place. With the first three we are already familiar.

Six Names for Certain Modes of Composition

Orav (5 notes). Under this head come all rags, ragnis, or putras which have five notes.

Sharav (6 notes). Under this head come all rags, ragnis, or putras which have six notes.

Sampooran (7 notes). Under this head come all rags, ragnis, or putras that have seven notes.

Shudh. All rags, ragnis, putras in which only naturals are used.[1]

Chhaya lagathoa. All rags, ragnis, putras into which another rag is introduced, which has only one sharp or flat, after which introduction the rag returns to its own form.

Sankiran. All rags, ragnis, putras into which two, three, or four other rags are introduced, each rag retaining its own laws and forms.

Under these six heads all rags, ragnis, and putras can be classified.

I believe the portraits of these six mighty rags with their mystical powers are to be seen in Bengal bazars. Bhairau the three-eyed, with a moon on his forehead, the Ganges flowing out of his head, encircled with serpents and wearing a necklace of skulls; Malkaus, a warrior surrounded by warriors; Hindola in his swinging cradle; Dipak shining in darkness; Sirirag dressed in scarlet and adorned with budding leaves; Megh clad in yellow and seated on a cloud. I have been able to obtain the portraits of some of their wives, the ragnis. But, although I lately came across a circumstantial list of these wives and their children, the putras, which I give for what it is worth in the form of genealogical tables, it must not be forgotten that the rags, like other gods of Olympia, were apparently 'to one thing constant never,' and have different ragnis apportioned to them in every province in which they are known, while we are told of still other ragnis called Amezzi or mixed ragnis 'which are of later growth and too numerous to detail.'

1. In his treatise on *The Musical Scales of the Hindus* Raja Tagore gives, under the head of Shudh, those rags 'which show the character of only one raga.'

BHAIRAU'S RAGNIS.

Bhairavin, Bilavoli, Ahi, Bangli, Aslekhi.

BHEROO'S PUTRAS.

Panchama, Harkh, Bisakh, Bangalam,
Madhu, Madhar, Laht, Bilaval.

MALKAUS'S RAGNIS.

Gorkari, Devgandhari, Gandhari, Sihuti, Dhanasari.

MALKAUS'S PUTRAS.

Maru, Mast, Angnevari, Prabalchand,
Kansok, Ubhara, Khokat, Bhanranad.

HINDOLA'S RAGNIS.

Telangi, Devkari, Basanti, Sandhur, Ahire.

HINDOLA'S PUTRAS.

Surmanand, Dhaskar, Chandarbimb, Savasbran,
Basant, Binoda, Kamoda.

DIPAK'S RAGNIS.

Kachheli, Patmangan, Todi, Kamodi, Gujri.

DIPAK'S PUTRAS.

Kalangi, Kuntla, Kamal, Kusian, Kawra,
Kaliani, Champak, Gawra.

SIRIRAG'S RAGNIS.

Bairare, Karndti, Gauri, Asavari, Sindhuri.

SIRIRAG'S PUTRAS.

Shahi, Sharag, Sagra, Gond, Gambhir,
Gond, Kumbh, Hamir.

Megh's Ragnis.
Sorath, Gond, Malari, Asa, Sahi.

Megh's Putras.
Baivadhar, Gajdhar, Kedara, Jablidhar,
Nut, Anjaldhara, Shankar, Shaina.

Hindu Tar

So much for the classification of the rag by educated musicians. Now we have to consider the question of time, as applied to the air played or sung along with its accompaniment on the drum. And this, to our English ears, is the most confusing and bewildering feature connected with Indian music. Taken separately we can follow either kind of time. But if, not content to enjoy the general impression produced by the two modes of counting, one attempts to analyse and to determine how the two parts belong to each other: where the drum-beat falls, often with irregular rhythm; and how its beat mates with the rhythm of the music : then at first, in my experience, everything appears most confusing. I can only compare it to the impression produced by the effort made by anyone to rub and pat himself at the same time, with the additional determination to accentuate some of the pats.

I shall tell you the little I have learnt from my labours to disentangle the puzzle.

No confusion reigns in the mind or methods of the musician. Laws and regulations are as rigidly laid down and observed in this department, as in every other of Indian music. But for us, the theory is so much easier to master than the application of it, that my advice to every beginner would be this: Work at theory and practice together. Master the established principles, find a drummer and singer who are gifted with patience, make them give you all the information they can, such as the name of the rag, the time of the drum-beat, which they call tal; make them play each of these separately and then together. After that slowly, laboriously, by dint of questions on your part, explanation on theirs, endless repetitions and ardent listening, you may arrive at an understanding of what at first appeared impossible to fathom.

One must remember in doing this, that the ordinary native musician is no more capable of sustained mental effort than most men of his class in any country. These lessons had better therefore be taken in short spells, or you will learn that the teacher's mother is dying, his home is on fire, or his own unexpected state of health or business affairs demands his return on that very day and hour to his own home!

On our side we should recollect that we now enter another world from our own, whose laws we must learn and accept, without, so far as I can see, being able to apply to them any of the accepted formulae of our own traditions.

Terms used in Counting Air and Drum-beat

And now to unravel the separate threads of the skein. We must in the first place grasp the fact that the drum-beat is counted in one way, the air in another. I shall give some of the terms used for these two modes of counting drum-beat and air. The terms I shall attempt to explain are:

Tal and Khali.

Vibhag, Ginti, and Matra.

Avard or Sam.

The first two are used in connexion with the time of the drum-beat. The next three in connexion with the time of the air. The last two are used when the performers are speaking of certain subdivisions of the rag (song or air), in each of which both of these modes of time are worked out together.

Terms used in connexion with the Time of the Drum-beat

Tal. The drummer beats on his two drums, sometimes with one hand, sometimes with both, and the beats to which he gives a peculiar emphasis, and which stand out from the rest, are called tal.

There are numerous varieties of tal. They have all their own names, of which I shall presently given a specimen list. Two of the best known are called tin-tal and char-tal. When a tal is called tin-tal, it means that three beats are given in certain subdivisions of the song, and the drummer continues to give these three beats at stated intervals, throughout each subdivision of the performance. If it is called char-tal, it means the emphasised beats are four, and so on. These beats are not easy to follow at first, as some of the intermediate notes on the drum are also accentuated, and when one is anxious to recognise and count the real beats, these extra intermediate thumps on the drum are disconcerting and misleading. The intervals between the beats, which we should call rests, are called *khali, i.e.* empty.

To give an example. 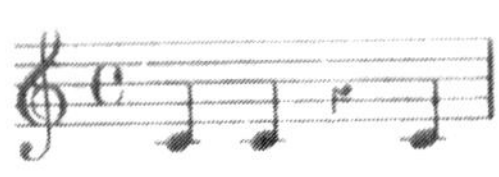 If beats occurred in this way in European music we should call the time common time, four in the bar; but the Hindus would call it tin-tal, because only three beats have been sounded, and the 'rest' they call *khali.*

Terms used in connexion with the Time of the Air

Vibhag. The song is divided into bars. The name for the bar is Vibhag.

Ginti. The word ginti (counting) is used when counting the time of the bars of the song.

Matra. Matra is the name given to the separate beats both in the bar and in further subdivision of the air. Matra may be described as a unit of time, generally a crotchet.

Subdivisions of the Rag

I must now explain what is meant by these subdivisions, to which I have referred when speaking both of tal and ginti.

The larger subdivisions of the airs are called avard, and this term is the most difficult to translate into English.

Avard. Avard means the sum total of the tal and the sum total of the ginti.

When both of these have been simultaneously completed the completion is called avard. In other words the drum-beat (tal) and beats counted in the bar (ginti) keep pace with one another. When a sufficient number of bars have been played or sung to let the drum-beats have time to work out their appointed number, then, bars and drum-beats being finished, the whole is called the avard, and a fresh avard begins.

A simple explanation was offered me by the illustration given of a circle, which is a second word used instead of avard. The spokes of the wheel are the counting in the bars of the rag (ginti), while the 1, 2, 3, 4 mark where the drum-beats come in. The whole circle is called the avard.

Sam. Sam is the name given to the point in the avard where the counting of the drum-beats (tal) begins. Sam is synonymous with the first beat of the tal.

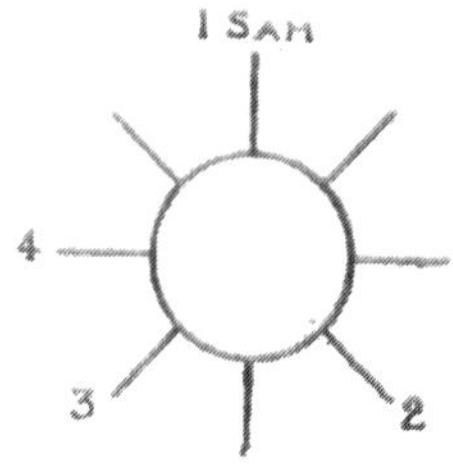

The circle may require many bars to give the drum-beats their opportunity. In that case you are told how many matras there are in each bar, and how many matra in the circle.

Matras Vibhag and Matra. To make a distinction between these two forms of matras, the phrase matras vibhag is used when referring to the matras in the bar. The word matra is employed by itself when referring to the matra in the circle. Pandit Vishnu Digambar, therefore, in the introduction which he gives to his airs in his primer, always states how many matra there are in the circle and uses the words matras vibhag for the matras used in the bar.

Number of Matras in Hindu Bars

A characteristic feature in Hindu music, for which we can find no equivalent in our own, is that while we count only multiples of 3 or 4 in our bars, they may also count 5, 7, or 9 in theirs, whether these be crotchets or quavers.

These irregularities are not so difficult to detect as might be imagined. This is what generally happens. You begin, when listening to some rag which is new to you, with the assumption that the time is regular, discover an odd note at the end of the bar you are counting, and conclude you have hit upon a specimen of 5, 7, or 9 time as the case may be. You then test your conclusion by identifying the extra note throughout the performance.

Classification of Matras used in a Bar

The following classification is given of every possible number of matras which may be in a bar. Under the head of chatasr comes every bar in which four is counted, or what we would call common time, whether semibreves, minims, or crotchets are used :

Tisr	has three, six, or nine matras in each bar.
Misr	has five or ten matras in each bar.
Kanda	has seven or fourteen matras in each bar.
Sankiran	has nine matras in each bar.

Always remember that, as I have said before, you must greatly depend upon applying yourself the principles you have learnt from educated musicians. Illiterate players ignorantly practise what the educated teach; they have a limited vocabulary in nomenclature;. they can give you the names of the notes, sa, re, ga, etc.; they beat with their hands these varied times of the ginti and tal; they know where the avard begins and ends; they give you the names of the tal, but they possibly might not understand what you meant if you used the words vibhag, ginti, matra, avard, still less if you spoke about chatasr, tisr, etc.; just as people might be able to speak grammatically, and as they had always been taught to speak, and yet be unable to parse the sentence. It may happen, to pursue the analogy that you have to teach your musician his parts of speech; but his sentence was correct grammar, although he had not learnt them.

To listen to these novelties in time is like hearing a new rhythm in poetry with a beauty all its own, elusive, fascinating, incommunicable. One can feel, too, in the same way the charm, the swing, the monotonous reiteration, the vociferous throb of the drum-beat, with the same sense of impotence and powerlessness to reproduce it. To follow the ginti is simplicity itself compared to the task of following the drum-beat (tal).

Perhaps you might find it some help, as I have done, in this connexion to learn a little of what one might call the language of the drum, although this language varies in different Provinces, just as the names given to the rags, ragnis, and the tals vary too.

Names for the Drum-beats

The Hindus have a name for each beat on the drum. Each tone is produced in its own place, whether on the edge, the inner side, or the centre, and certain fingers are used to produce the tone. A Punjab drummer gave me the following names for his drum-beats:

Da is the name of a stroke given by the first finger.
Din is a stroke given by the first and second finger together.
Na is a stroke given by the first finger.
Trik is a stroke given by the first, second, and third together.
Ka is a stroke given by the second and third together.
Kut is a stroke given by the second and third together.
Ta is a stroke given by the first finger.
Tin is a stroke given by the first and second together.

While they give these strokes they repeat with its appropriate amount of accent the name of the stroke. Da *dinak, trik* ka, *kut* ta, *tin* ta.

Sometimes both hands strike the drum, sometimes only one. Both hands invariably contribute the beat. The right hand generally devotes itself to the intermediate ornamentation, so it is more important to watch the left hand in following the beat. As a drummer once said to me, 'the beat is like the seam of my coat—that must be there; the other notes are like the embroidery I may put according to my own fancy over the seam.' Here is an example of char-tal. I have put a cross (x) where the beat comes, and accent circumflex (>) where the disturbing intermediate accent falls:

		>		>	x	>		>
Right hand :	**Da**	**Din**	**Din**	**Da**	**Da**	**Din**	**Din**	**Da**
Left hand :	**Da**				**Da**	**Din**	**Din**	**Da**

Here is another example of char-tal:

Right hand :	**Din Din Da**	**trik ka tunah**	**kutta a Din**	**trikka Dunna**
Left hand :	**Din Din Da**		**Din**	**Din**

A young Hindu who had learnt the principles of the Hindu system of music wrote the drum-beats of tin-tal in this way, explaining that there were eight matra in the circle, and that the beat came on the first, third, and seventh of these, which he also understroked.

(1)	(2)	(3)	(4)
Deva Din	**Dhin Dha**	***Deva Dhin***	**Din Dha**
(5)	**(6)**	**(7)**	**(8)**
Ta Tin	**Tin Ta**	***Dhera Dhin***	**Dhin Dha**

And this is how he wrote Jhap tal, in which there were ten matra in the circle, the beat falling on the first, third, and eighth.

(1)	(2)	(3)	(4)	(5)	(6)	(7)	(8)	(9)	(10)
Dhi	na	*Dhi*	Dhi	na	Ti	na	*Dhi*	Dhi	na

List of the Tals

On the following page I give a diagram, with a list of the names of the tals and their analysis.

Although these are the names and measures of generally known tals, you must not be surprised if you cannot classify the tals you hear under any of these heads.

Every Indian musician may invent his own tal, provided only that, having started it according to his own conception, he maintains the same number of tals throughout.

If he has 7 tals in the first avard for instance, and has fixed the intervals there ought to be between the tals, then he must stick to 7 tals with these intervals throughout the performance.

If he boasts of a drummer as an accompanist, he sings his song, the drummer listens and calculates how many matra there are in the avard, and then arranges how many tal there should be to suit them. Woe betide the singer who has picked up some stray drummer who is not in sympathy with him, for he has it in his power to spoil the rhythm of all the improvised flights by beating out of time with their character, just as any bungler might reduce the best efforts of a prima donna to absurdity by striking chords at inappropriate moments. Some examples are given of Indian airs in European notation, to illustrate how the drum-beats fall and the principle of the avard. The airs have 5 and 7 crotchets in the bar.

Ancient name of tal	Modern name	Matra	Tal	Khali	Vibhag	Vibhag matras
Ganamantha .	Titala	8	tin	1	2	4
Abhi narda .	Surfakata	10	tin	2	2	5
"	Jhap tal	10	tin	1	2	5
Chachaput .	Chau tala	12	char	2	2	3
Ratilila . .	Drutcha tal	6	char	2	2	3
Araswati kantha .	Adachautala	14	char	3	2	7
"	Jhumbra	14	tin	1	2	7
"	Dhamar	14	tin	1	2	7
Tribhinna .	Dipchandi or Chanchal	7	tin	1	2	3½
"	Rupak or Dhaital	7	tin	1	1	7
"	Tevra or Tal	7	tin	1	1	7
"	Savari	15	char	3	3	5
Prati Manthaka	Dadara velambit	3	do	1	1	3
Dar-pana .	Dadara drut	3	ek	1	1	3
Yati tal . .	Kerava	2	ek	1	1	3
Dhanan-jaya	Kavali or Dhumathi	4	tin	1	2	2

Specimen of Air with Seven Crotchets in the Bar

This air is orav, *i.e.* five notes are used in it. The tal is tevra, the drum-beat marked by the numerals 1, 2, 3 falls on the first, fourth, and sixth crotchet in the bar. I have put a crotchet rest where the drum-beat is omitted (khali). The avard is completed in one bar. The Alapa (introduction) has its own time.

Specimen of Air with Five Crotchets in the Bar.

Tal surfakata: the drum-beat falling on the first, second, and second half of the fourth crotchet. The avard is completed in two bars.

Specimen of Air with Seven Quavers in the Bar.

Tal rupak or Dhaital: the drum-beat falling on the first, third, and seventh quavers in the bar. The avard is completed in one bar.

Hindu Airs

Hindu airs are short, and are generally composed of four parts. First comes the Alankar, an improvised introduction, in which all the notes to be used are given. Then comes the first division of the air, called Astai, followed by the second, called Antara. The musician always returns to the Astai, and ends with its conclusion. The air is seldom repeated in the same way. A long abbreviation is often introduced, called the Alapa, which is like the insertion of two additional lines of poetry into a poem, the measure of the accompaniments remaining the same throughout.

Words sung to Airs

As to the literary merits of the words sung to the airs, I am not in a position to judge, through ignorance of the subject. One realises the extent of that ignorance, and the presumption it would be to generalise on such a theme, when one reads the mere epitome of the poetry and songs of India given by Raja Tagore, which is like perusing the catalogue of a library of books, written in some unknown tongue.

Not many Europeans, I fancy, would boast of being even superficially acquainted with the Dhrupada style of song: the popular Tappas; the Thumri songs of the North-West Provinces; the Kharkhas or war songs of the Rajputs; the Huttari chants, the nursery rhymes, the wedding and cremation songs of the people of Coorg; the Zicree songs of Guzrat : the Vernams, Pathams, Kirthanas of Madras. Few have read the 'Cural,' which is considered 'the literary treasure, the poetic mouthpiece, the highest type of verbal and moral excellence amongst the Tamil people,' or the Chandi, Ramayana, and Kabi songs of Bengal. Who amongst us know the lyric poetry of Vidyapati of Chandidas, Jayadeva, or of the well-known family of Rambagan Dutt, sometimes called 'the nest of singing birds'? Besides these there are countless others which need not be enumerated here.

Personally I have to confess, that in the one small corner which is all I know of the vast Empire of India, I have only heard some cradle, love, and marriage songs, one or two dirges, one or two songs of Krishna, some ballads of the loves of Hir and Ranjha, of Leila and Majnu, one or two religious poems, a few Ghazals, the songs sung by Mirasi which are supposed to be of Persian origin. Of these I have read the literal translations of perhaps fifty, and the originals of little more than half-a-dozen.

Any opinion I may therefore hazard on these must be taken for the little it is worth. The best of them, so far as I can judge from my very limited experience, have the pith and terseness, the human notes of elemental joy and sorrow which are to be found in the folksongs of all countries; with an indigenous flavour all their own. Others again seem to be as elliptical as the proverbs of the Punjab, which leave the central incident to be inferred, like the instance of American humour given in the account of the death of a child: 'Two boys played at William Tell and the apple. The funeral was the largest ever seen in New York.' Indeed, so disjointed are the ideas in some of the songs I have read, that one is reminded of the game in which one person writes a line of poetry, folds up the paper and hands it to his neighbour to continue as he pleases, only furnishing him with the last word with which he has to rhyme.

In the cradle songs, the language and ideas are very much what is understood between mothers and their babies all the world over. In the popular love songs certain similes, such as comparing the loved one's locks to snakes, the songster's bed to thorns and fire, are much favoured, while the prosaic joys of eating are as frankly introduced into the most fervent, as beer and sausages into the classical smoking concerts of Germany. In the religious poems alone does the spiritualising idealism of our own love-songs apparently find a place. The area which I have traversed, however, is extremely limited. Here and there one comes upon bits of pure gold amongst the earthly dross, meriting further search. More, no doubt, are to be found in regions hitherto unknown to me, where those who have the patience and faithfulness to seek, may be rewarded by discovering nuggets.

The makers of such music must have it in them to write songs. I only know how beautiful their music often is, and so again I would urge others to follow on the road, which I have dimly indicated, and to learn to know that music for themselves, and all the more because, apart from its own inherent beauty, I believe that knowing it they will learn to know and understand the people amongst whom they live.

'The study of music,' writes Raja Tagore, with a curious confirmation of Sir Hubert Parry's views on the same subject, 'is important to the musician from an ethnological point of view, as it affords him an insight into the inward man and displays the character and temperament of different races and the relations which they bear to one another....'

'The shepherd tending his flock, the fisherman mending his net, the labourer in the paddy field, the cartman drawing his cart, has no inducement to sing his favourite tune unless he is prompted by the emotions of his heart...National music means a faithful expression of national feelings.'

Pierre Loti, in his account of his visit to India, ends a chapter on Indian music with these words: 'Cet orchestre, ces chanteurs appartiennent au Maharajah....Oh! combien doit être loin de la nôtre la rêverie de ce prince, et sa conception des tristesses de l'amour, des tristesses de la mort! Mais cette musique distinguée et rare, qui est la sienne, me révèle un peu de son âme, mieux sans doute que nos courts entretiens, corrects, gênés de cérémonial et de mots étrangers.'

In concluding my inadequate attempt to explain the system of Indian music, may I again express the hope that my countrymen may be encouraged to continue the study for themselves? For I am convinced that they will find a reward for all their labours in the pleasure attending the pursuit.

GLOSSARY

ABHI NANDA, ancient name of a tal.

ADACHAUTALA, modern name of a tal.

AHI, name of a ragni.

AHIRE, name of a ragni.

ALANKAR, an introduction to an air.

ALAPA, an improvised interlude in an air.

ANGNEVARI, name of a putra.

ANJALDHARA, name of a ragni.

ANTARA, second division of an air.

ANU-DRUT, name for a semiquaver.

ANU-ANUDRUT, name for a demi-semiquaver.

ANUVADI, note subordinate to principal note.

ARASWANTI KANTHA, ancient name of a tal.

ARCHIK, name given to a composition in which one note is used.

AROHA, ascending.

ASAVARI, name of a ragni.

ASA, name of a ragni.

ASLEKHI, name of a ragni.

ASTAI, first division of an air.

ATTI KOMAL, name for a quarter-note.

AVARD, name given to certain sub-divisions of rag.

AVAROHA, descending.

BAIVADHAR, name of a putra.

BANGALAM, name of a putra.

BANGLI, name of a ragni.

BASANT, name of a putra.

BASANTI, name of a ragni.

BHAIRAU, name of a rag.

BHAIRAVIN, name of a ragni.

BILAVAL, name of a putra.

BINODA, name of a putra.

BISAKH, name of a putra.

CHACHAPUT, ancient name of a tal.

CHANCHAL, modern name of a tal.

CHANDARBIMB, name of a putra.

CHAMPAK, name of a putra.

CHATASR, name of a semibreve.

CHATASR, name for a bar of music in which four is counted.

CHAU TALA, modern name of a tal.

CHHAYA LAGATHOA, a name for a certain mode of composition.

DADARA, modern name of a tal.

DADARA DRUT, modern name of a tal.

DAR-PANA, ancient name of a tal.

DEVGANDHARI, name of a ragni.

DEVKARI, name of a ragni.

DHA, abbreviated name for the note corresponding to our A.

DHAITAL, modern name of a tal.

DHAIVATA, name for the note corresponding to our A.

DHAMAR, modern name of a tal.

DHANAN-JAVA, ancient name of a tal.

DHANASARI, name of a ragni.

DHASKAR, name of a putra.

DHOL, species of drum.

DHOLKI, species of drum.

DHUMATHI, modern name of a tal.

DIPAK, name of a rag.

DIPCHANDI, modern name of a tal.

DRUT, pace in Indian music corresponding to our presto.

DRUT, name of a quaver.

DRUTCHA TAL, modern name of a tal.

DUGAN, pace in Indian music corresponding to our moderato.

GA, abbreviated name for the note corresponding to our E.

GAJDHAR, name of a putra.

GAMBHIR, name of a putra.

GANDHAR, name of the note corresponding to our E.

GANDHARI, name of a ragni.

GANAMANTHA, ancient name of a tal.

GATIK, name given to Hindu musical composition when only two notes are used.

GAURI, name of a ragni.

GAWRA, name of a putra.

GHAZAL, song supposed to be of Persian origin.

GINTI, counting.

GIT, song.

GOND, name of a putra.

GORKARI, name of a ragni.

GRAMA, name for certain scales.

GUJRI, name of a ragni.

GURU, name of a minim.

HAMIR, name of a putra.

HARKH, name of a putra.

HINDOLA, name of a rag.

HIR and RANJHA, hero and heroine of a well-known ballad.

JABLIDHAR, name of a putra.

KACHHELI, name of a ragni.

KALANGI, name of a putra.

KALIAM, the name of a putra.

KALIANI, name of a putra.

KAMAL, name of a putra.

KAMODA, name of a putra.

KANDA, name of a bar of music in which seven or fourteen is counted.

KANSOK, name of a putra.

KARNDTI, name of a ragni.

KAVALI, modern name of a tal.

KAWRA, name of a putra.

KEDARA, name of a putra.

KERAVA, modern name of a tal.

KHALI, empty.

KHARJA (SHUDJA), Hindu name for the note corresponding to our C.

KHOKAT, name of a putra.

KOMAL, Sanskrit name for a semi-tone.

KUMBH, name of a putra.

KUNTLA, name of a putra.

KUSIAN, name of a putra.

LAGHU, name of a crotchet.

LAHT, name of a putra.

MA, abbreviated name for the note corresponding to our F.

MADHAR, name of a putra.

MADHU, name of a putra.

MADHYA, name for tenor.

MADHYAMA, name for the note corresponding to our F.

MALKAUS, name of a rag.

MALARI, name of a ragni.

MANDRA, name for bass.

MARU, name of a putra.

MAST, name of a putra.

MATRA, name given to separate beats in a bar of music.

MEGH, name of a rag.

MIRASI, Mohammedan bard-musician.

MISR, name of bar of music in which five or ten is counted.

MURCHHANA, name given to a vibration on a note in singing or to a run from one note to another.

NAWAB, a Mohammedan prince or noble.

Ni, abbreviated name for note corresponding to our B.

NISHADA, name for note corresponding to our B.

NUT, name of a putra.

ORAV, name given to a composition in which six notes are used.

PA, abbreviated name of note corresponding to our G.

PANCHAMA, name of note corresponding to our G.

PANCHAMA, name of a putra.

PATMANGAN, name of a ragni.

PRABALCHAND, name of a putra.

PRATI MANTHAKA, ancient name of a tal.

PUTRAS, airs connected with ragnis and rags.

RAG, a certain form of musical composition.

RAGNIS, airs connected with rags.

RATILILA, ancient name of a tal.

RE, abbreviated name of note corresponding to our D.

RISHABA, name of note correspond-ing to our D.

RUPAK, modern name of a tal.

SA, abbreviated name of note corresponding to our C.

SAGRA, name of a putra.

SAHI, name of a ragni.

SAM, name given to certain sub-divisions of the rag.

SAMIK, name given to compositions in which three notes are used.

SAMPOORAN, name given to compositions in which seven notes are used.

SAMVADI, harmony.

SANDHUR, name of a ragni.

SANKIRAN, name of bar of music in which nine is counted.

SANKIRAN, name of a certain formation of rags, ragnis, and putras.

SAPTAKA, name of the Indian scale or octave.

SARANGI, musical instrument resembling a violin.

SAVASBRAN, name of a putra.

SAVARI, name of a putra.

SHAHI, name of a putra.

SHAINA, name of a putra.

SHANKAR, name of a putra.

SHARAG, name of a putra.

SHARAV, name given to compositions in which six notes are used.

SHUDH, name for a natural in music.

SHUDH, name for certain formation of rags, ragnis, and putras.

SHUDJA, Hindu name for the note corresponding to our C.

SIHUTI, name of a ragni.

SINDHURI, name of a ragni.

SIRIRAG, name of a rag.

SITAR, musical instrument resembling a violin.

SONI and MAIWAL, hero and heroine of an Indian ballad.

SORATH, name of a ragni.

SRUTIS, quarter-notes in octave.

SURFAKATA, modern name of a tal.

SURMANAND, name of a putra.

SWAR, a whole tone in octave.

SWARANTER, name given to compositions in which only four notes are used.

TABLUS, a species of drum.

TAL, name for principal beats given by the drum.

TAMBOURA, musical instrument resembling a violin.

TAR, name for treble.

TELANGI, name of a ragni.

TIBRE, name for quarter-note before a sharp.

TIBRE TAR, name for sharp.

TIBRE TAM, name for quarter-note above a sharp.

TISR, name of bar of music in which six or nine is counted.

TITALA, modern name of a tal.

TODI, name of a ragni.

TRIBHINNA, ancient name of a tal.

UBHARA, name of a putra.

UNVADI, name for a chord.

VADI, name given to the principal note in a composition.

VELAMBIT, pace in music correponding to our adagio.

VIBHAG, name corresponding to our bar in music.

VINA, ancient musical instrument resembling a violin.

VIVADI, discordant.

YATI TAL, ancient name of a tal.